The Ultimate Guide to Purchasing Florida Real Estate

by:

Buck Boyles

&

Preston Boyles

www.marlin-realty.com

Copyright © 2014 Ottis "Buck" Boyles Jr. & Preston Boyles

Marlin Realty & Investments, Inc.

All rights reserved.

ISBN: 1502859734
ISBN-13: 978-1502859730

INTRODUCTIONS

The Principals at Marlin Realty & Investments, Inc. have over 40 years of combined experience in developing, building and selling Florida real estate. Over the last 40 years we've seen people who invest in Florida real estate make huge profits, with many becoming millionaires while others "lose their shirts". We've seen interest rates as high as twenty percent and less than four percent. We've seen markets so "hot" that people were lined up to purchase property and other markets so slow that the phone simply didn't ring.

We've seen it all. That's why we decided to create this guide. Being in the real estate brokerage business, we want everyone to make a profit. Referrals from satisfied customers are the backbone of any real estate brokerage business, therefore this guide has been written primarily for the individual or small investment group that doesn't have access to resources that help determine the value or risk involved in purchasing real estate. We understand that large companies, developers and retailers can afford to do demographic studies, hire researchers, develop computer models and take advantage of information that the man on the street or small investor doesn't have.

We are going to take the "common sense" approach and provide information that you probably won't get anywhere else. Hopefully this information will help you make wise and profitable decisions. We're not recommending any particular type of real estate investment. That will be determined by your particular financial requirements and investment goals. Real estate has historically been a pretty safe and profitable investment for individuals who do the research and gather the knowledge necessary to make intelligent choices.

Good luck with your real estate investments.

Disclaimer: **Marlin Realty & Investments, Inc. is not a law firm. We do not practice law. The information contained in the booklet is general in nature, is based on our past experience and is not intended to be legal advice. When addressing legal issues, the reader should seek proper legal advice from an attorney.**

The Ultimate Guide to Purchasing Florida Real Estate

Marlin Realty & Investments, Inc.

CONTENTS

	Introductions	iii
1	Why Purchase Florida Real Estate?	1
2	Establish Your Investment Goals	15
3	Take "Emotion" Out of Your Investment	19
4	Location! Location! Location!	23
5	Mistakes People Make	33
6	Foreign Investors	39
7	Types of Investments	43
8	Financing	49
9	Professional Assistance	55
10	Questions Most Often Asked	65
	About the Authors	73

1

WHY PURCHASE FLORIDA REAL ESTATE?

There are many valid reasons to invest in Florida Real Estate. Florida is one of the fastest growing states in the country. It is ranked number four in population behind California, Texas, and New York. And some census estimates are saying that the state will soon be ranked number three. The 2008 population was estimated to be around eighteen million, an increase of a little over five million since 1990. It is projected to continue that growth at least through 2025. Already there are strong signs that the more affluent "baby boomers" are making Florida a chosen destination – and this wave of retirees is not expected to flatten out until the early 2020's. Even if the "baby boomer" influx flattens out, it is estimated that foreign-born real estate purchasers are likely to offset any downturn in demand following the baby-boomer generation and are expected to rise steadily, based on recent significant immigration increases. Young families are also moving into the state because more companies are relocating to Florida which will over time significantly increase the job opportunities.

With a rapid population growth, it's pretty obvious that these new residents have to have a place to live which means new homes, condos and apartments. New residents create a need for more commercial and retail development as well as medical services, entertainment, and educational facilities, etc. Each of these areas presents real estate investment opportunities.

Florida is often referred to as the "Gateway to the Carribean and Latin America" and with good reason. Forty percent of all U.S. exports to Latin and South America pass through Florida.

In addition to rapid population increases, Florida offers 663 miles of beaches, mild year round climate, 1,197 miles of coastline, 7,700 lakes greater than 10 acres, 12 International Airports, 14 deep water Ports, 11,000 miles of rivers and streams, 1,250 golf courses (more than any other state), and World renowned tourist destinations such as Disney World, EPCOT, NASA Kennedy Space Center, Everglades National Park, Busch Gardens, Sea World, Daytona Speedway, and Universal Studios. Florida is the top tourist destination in the world which requires a tremendous support infrastructure. That infrastructure creates a lot of investment opportunities. The tourist business which has an economic impact of over $57 billion on Florida's economy also creates a lot of jobs.

Tourism is Florida's leading industry, employing around one million people and accounting for more than one-fifth of the state's sales tax revenue. And, the tourist industry is expected to continue to grow. The Florida Panhandle beaches have experienced a stunning post-oil-spill rebound and have become a bright spot for the tourist industry.

The space industry represents over $4.5 billion of the state's economy. The number of employees at the Kennedy Space Center is approximately 15,000 and Florida ranks 4th among the states in overall aerospace employment. The space center employment numbers will change as the government turns over much of the space program to private enterprise.

Florida also leads the southeast in farm income and produces 75% of the U.S. oranges and accounts for about 40% of the world's orange juice supply. Few people know this but Florida is also known internationally for raising, training and selling horses. The city of Ocala in central Florida is officially recognized by the Department of Agriculture as "The Horse Capital of The World". More than 200 farms and training centers in this area are devoted to breeding, training and showing breeds such as Thoroughbreds, Pasco Fino, Missouri Foxtrotter, Arabian, Morgan, miniature horse, quarter horse, hunter/jumper and draft horses among others. Nearly 29,000 people are employed in the area's Thoroughbred industry. The Thoroughbred industry's economic impact on the state is considered to be in excess of $1 billion dollars annually and the horse sales at the Ocala Breeder's Sales Complex run into the millions.

Florida has a strong economy and **no personal income tax**. Florida ranks low in terms of the tax burden placed on residents. Based on income, property and other state and local tax collections, the Tax

Foundation research organization ranks Florida among the lowest tax states with only five states having a lower tax burden. Florida's Homestead Exemption Law offers a big savings for a Florida homeowner when he declares the home his permanent residence.

Marlin Realty & Investments, Inc.

AND don't forget one of the main reasons many people want to move to Florida – <u>great</u> <u>weather</u>. Listed below are the average annual temperatures for the major cities.

City	Average Low	Average High
Daytona	61	80
Fort Lauderdale	67	84
Fort Meyers	64	84
Jacksonville	59	79
Key West	73	83
Miami	69	83
Orlando	62	83
Pensacola	59	77
Tallahassee	56	79
Tampa	63	82
West Palm Beach	67	83

Recently the Florida government has come to the realization that they cannot solely rely on Florida's location and good weather to bring in new residents. They realize that you also need a strong employment base. Therefore there is now a movement toward a reduction of regulations and the introduction of incentives to make the state more attractive to businesses who desire to relocate to the state. There are also efforts being made to improve the education system which will further encourage families to relocate to Florida.

Baring a national catastrophe, Florida has to be one of the top growth states in the country over the next few decades. Real estate investment opportunities should be almost unlimited.

Marlin Realty & Investments, Inc.

2

ESTABLISH YOUR INVESTMENT GOALS

If you don't have a plan or you don't know what your goals are, you should not be investing in real estate. You might as well take you money to Las Vegas and take your chances. The advantage in setting investment goals is it gives you an opportunity to develop a plan through which you can measure results.

You have to determine if your goal is to create a short term or long term real estate investment or possibly both. A short term investment will usually involve purchasing a home or vacant land or lot at a low price and then flip it (sell) in a short time hopefully at a profit. Short term investments usually involve a lot of risk because you are gambling that the property you purchase is going to quickly increase in value. Short term investments require a lot of research and knowledge of the local real estate markets and timing is critical.

Real estate markets historically go up and down. We have had a real estate recession of some degree in the United States approximately every seven years since World War II. During a real estate "boom" as we experienced a short time back, prices were going up so fast that builders were raising their prices as often as once a week. Investors were buying and building homes at a frantic pace and flipping them at a profit. People were buying vacant lots and reselling them in a very short time and doubling or tripling the price. Investors were purchasing condominiums at a discount while they were still under construction and flipping them at a profit to other investors who flipped them again at a profit before construction was finished. Money was easy to get and lenders were loaning money to people with poor credit or no credit.

Those kinds of "hot" markets can never sustain themselves because prices keep going up to a point where investors can no longer flip properties at a profit and people simply get priced out of the market. An unrealistic market is created, everything levels off and prices usually start going down which creates a real estate recessionary period. The people who get hurt in these markets are the one's who purchase at the top of the market or near the end of the "boom" period.

Short term investments usually involve buying real estate at "bargain" prices, holding for a relatively short period and then selling at a profit. These types of investments will require cash because you have to be prepared to move quickly when opportunities arise and financing will be much more difficult to obtain.

If you want to be successful with short term real estate investments, you have to get on the right side of the "wave". As a general rule, you buy when prices are going down and you sell when prices are going up. You never wait to see where the "bottom" of the market is or where the "top" of the market is. It is impossible to know where the top or bottom of a real estate market is until after it is reached and heads in the other direction. We hear these "words of wisdom" all the time. "Last year I could have sold my property for twenty or thirty thousand dollars more." "Last year I could have purchased this property for twenty or thirty thousand dollars less." Why didn't these people sell or buy last year? They got greedy and tried to wait for the top or bottom of the market and they lost. **You have to stay on the right side of the "wave".**

A long term investment usually involves less risk and could be a single family home that you plan to live in or rent over an extended period of time, an apartment complex, strip shopping center or other type of commercial property. A long term investment can be income producing or you can simply hold it for long term appreciation in value such as well located vacant land.

There are some significant advantages in investing in real estate over other types of investments. Real estate investments have relatively high-yield possibilities, there are tax advantages, money can be leveraged and you can maintain a certain amount of personal control over the money invested.

Although real estate offers higher than average yields, the down side is that it requires a higher degree of personal control. A personal commitment to getting involved in management; whether you hire professional assistance or not, is crucial to your success. We can site many examples where investors bought homes to rent, turned them over to a management company and then found the home completely destroyed after a year.

There are many "so called" real estate management companies out there who do little more than collect rent. Their only interest is in collecting a fee. They do little screening of tenants and will rent to almost anyone who can breathe. We have seen homes that have been turned into marijuana "grow houses" by tenants. Walls have been removed, electrical wiring has been changed in an attempt to hide the excessive electric use, high powered heat lamps installed and 50 gallon drums filled with water to increase humidity have been placed throughout the home. Needless to say, the mold and mildew along with everything else totally destroys the interior of the homes leading to major renovations. Obviously in these cases, there was no management involved although a management company was being paid.

When renting to anyone, the lease should be prepared by an attorney and should spell out the responsibilities of the landlord and tenant. The lease should allow the landlord or the management company to inspect the premises at least monthly and it should allow for a quick removal of the tenant when the tenant violates the conditions of the lease. Also remember that the tenant has rights. A landlord would be wise to familiarize himself with the Florida Landlord Tenant law.

When dealing with a management company, a management contract should be prepared by <u>the landlord's</u> attorney spelling out the responsibilities of all parties. Remember, it's still the landlord's responsibility to oversee the management company.

Developing a plan, doing the research, and getting professional help minimizes the risk and maximizes the rewards.

3

TAKE "EMOTION" OUT OF YOUR INVESTMENT

When you purchase a home for your personal use, is it an investment? It better be, because it is usually the biggest single investment that a family will make during their lifetime. We have found that most families put little thought into what the resale value of their home might be after living in it for a few years. Too many families purchase a home with the idea that they are going to spend the rest of their lives in that home so they make a quick emotional decision without doing their homework.

The fact is; the average family in Florida lives in a house 6 to 7 years. If you purchase a home today, what is it going to be worth in seven years? Is it going to go up in value or go down? A lot of very nice homes are located in declining neighborhoods. The home might be beautiful and just what you're looking for but the neighborhood might be declining in value because of a new highway location or the homes in the surrounding area may be very old or a new shopping mall could have been built on the other side of town and everything is moving in that direction. There are a number of reasons why homes in a given neighborhood can go down in value. It pays to take the time to thoroughly check out the area.

We often see emotion in the form of **greed** heavily involved in decisions to purchase real estate. During the recent Florida real estate "boom", we saw many decisions made strictly on the basis of greed. Common sense didn't enter the picture. For example, there is an area in the west central part of Florida called Citrus Springs that was developed over fifty years ago. It is an area of approximately 15,000 acres that was subdivided into 33,500 residential building lots with 450 miles of paved streets. These lots were marketed all over the world at prices starting at around $1,200 per lot. Lots could be financed with a very low down payment. There was a lot of "hype" by well known sport figures and thousands of people flocked to the area and purchased over a million dollars worth of lots in one day with the idea that they would go up quickly in value as homes were built and the area developed.. **The opposite actually happened.**

Since Citrus Springs was developed in an area of Florida that was considered rather remote at the time and because most of the people who purchased the lots purchased with the idea of reselling them at a profit, very few people built homes, therefore Citrus Springs was very slow to develop. Instead of lot values going up, they actually went down over the years. Until the recent real estate "boom", a Citrus Springs lot could be purchased for as low as five hundred dollars or less.

At the beginning of the recent real estate "boom" a millionaire real estate investor went into Citrus Springs and purchased several hundred lots at less than five thousand dollars a lot. He knew that the real estate values were going up and he was gambling that the low priced lots he purchased would go up substantially in value. They did go up in value and he made a huge profit. When the word got out as to what the investor had done, other investment groups ran in to try to also purchase low priced lots. It started a "frenzy" of buying and selling. People were buying lots and flipping them to other investors at double what they paid for them. Everyone tried to get a "piece of the action". Greed dictated everything. Real estate salespeople advised people to "grab your lot before they're gone." Lot prices were driven up to $35,000 to $40,000 per lot. There was no reason for it except greed. After the bottom fell out of the market, lot prices in Citrus Springs dropped back down to as low as $1,000 per lot or less. Since there are currently approximately 30,000 vacant lots in Citrus Springs, the people who bought lots at the high prices are stuck. It may be years before the market allows them to just break even.

After reading about Citrus Springs, you may have the question: How would I determine the value of a lot located in an unfamiliar area? There is an old rule that builders and insurance companies have used for a long time. It's the 80/20 rule. When you build a home, you shouldn't put more than twenty percent of the total value into the land. Using that rule, if the average home in a given subdivision is selling for $100,000., then the lot should be worth around $20,000. The 80/20 rule is just a general rule to use to give you an idea of lot values. Obviously there will be a lot of exceptions. If you buy a home on the beach, the lot value might be higher than the value of the home.

We've seen a lot of people make emotional decisions to purchase commercial real estate and business opportunities. Everyone who buys or starts a restaurant business feels that their food is going to be better than everyone else's and people will flock to their location. This usually doesn't happen and most owners find out too late that not everyone likes their menu or their location or their lack of parking or their facility. They were so emotionally sure that their menu was going to be a hit that they forgot about doing proper planning. That's one of the reasons the restaurant business has the highest failure rate of any business in the country.

We recently worked with a couple of individuals who inherited a Bowling Alley business from their father. They had no experience in running a business but they were so emotionally involved in the business because their father started it that they refused to sell and attempted to run it themselves. When the country went into a recession, a lot of people stopped spending on recreation and the Bowling Alley business dropped dramatically. Instead of selling, the owners started paying the bills with their personal credit cards. That turned into a disaster and they were eventually forced to sell at a "give-a-way" price.

You also should remember that you will come across sellers who get emotionally attached to the property that they are selling and sometimes to the point that they will be totally unrealistic. We have seen sellers who received many fair and reasonable offers to purchase their property but they simply wouldn't budge an inch on the price. This type of seller usually has to have his property sit on the market for a long period before reality sets in and the price is lowered.

The whole point is, don't get caught up in the emotion of the moment, **do your homework and be realistic.**

4

LOCATION! LOCATION! LOCATION!

You hear this over and over when real estate is discussed. The three most important things to consider when purchasing real estate are location, location and location. Florida is a huge state with several hundred miles of coastline. It's approximately 850 miles from Key West to the western part of the Florida panhandle. Since Florida is such a long state, it offers a variety of elevations, terrain and climate temperatures. We're going to give you general information about Florida which should help you determine what locations would best fit your needs.

Because most of Florida was once under the sea, the majority of the state sits on a bed of limestone. The limestone is porous and contains an underground river called the Florida Aquifer. The Florida Aquifer starts in the Okefenokee Swamp in South Georgia and flows south underneath Florida and exits in the Gulf of Mexico around the Naples/Ft. Meyers area. This river provides a lot of the fresh water for Florida.

Since the limestone base is porous, there is always a chance that there could be a sinkhole anywhere in Florida so let's address that issue right now. Sinkholes are created when an open space in the limestone collapses and surface soil falls into the cavity and a hole is created at the surface. Sinkhole activity is usually minor and is not considered to be dangerous to humans. We only know of three deaths associated with sinkhole activity in Florida's history and two of those individuals were working with drilling equipment that collapsed. Your chance of getting struck with lighting is much greater that getting injured by a sinkhole. However, sinkholes can create cracks in foundations and walls. The State of Florida and several other Insurance Companies have special policies that address sinkhole activity.

When one is investing in a home or building in Florida, we would always recommend a building inspection to check for cracks, settlement damage, Chinese drywall and general condition. If you're purchasing a new home with a standard new home warranty, then you would probably not need a building inspection because the new home would have to meet all the current building codes and any defects would be covered by the warranty.

Land along Florida's coastline and all of the area roughly from Orlando south is considered a flood prone area because it is usually just a few feet above sea level. We went through a period during the eighty's and ninety's when there were very few hurricanes. As a result, some local governments got lax in their requirements and allowed some communities to be developed with inadequate drainage systems. It is not unusual for Florida to get 6 inches or more of rain in one day during the rainy season. Several years ago the Ft. Lauderdale area got 13 inches of rain in one day. You can imagine the flood problems those communities without adequate drainage experienced during those types of rainfalls.

How do you determine what communities have experienced flooding problems? As we said before, put your emotions aside and do your research. Ask people who reside in the area if they have had any flood problems. They usually won't hesitate to tell you if there have been problems because they are usually already mad at the local government for not requiring adequate drainage in the first place. Don't rely on the seller or a real estate salesperson to give you that information.

The north part of the state is less prone to flooding because the elevations are much higher. There are areas with elevations from 50 feet to 345 feet above sea level. There are places in northwest Florida that have elevations of 100 to 200 feet above sea level within a 15 minute drive of the Gulf of Mexico.

Hurricanes are a natural occurring phenomenon that Florida residents have to deal with every year. This scares a lot of people but let's put it in the proper prospective. Everywhere you live in the country, you have to deal with some kind of potential natural disaster. California has earthquakes and wildfires, the Southwest has droughts, the Midwest has tornados, the North has blizzards and other places have severe floods. If you want to live in Florida, you have to deal with hurricanes; however, there are locations in Florida that offer better protection from hurricanes than others and there are steps you can take to protect yourself and your property.

With the exception of the northwest Florida panhandle, historically the north half of Florida has had far fewer hits from hurricanes than the south half. The reason for that is the fact that most hurricanes travel from southeast to northwest. They typically go though the Caribbean and enter the Gulf of Mexico by crossing over Cuba or the southern part of Florida and continue west toward Texas, Mississippi, Louisiana and the west Gulf region. Occasionally a hurricane will turn north along the east coast of Florida and eventually strike the southeast part of the U.S.

If you want safety and protection from hurricanes for yourself and your property, it is wise to avoid low lying areas. The most severe damage from hurricanes is usually caused by flooding. If you are unsure as to whether you are in a low lying area subject to flooding, just check with a local insurance agency and they can look up the address and tell you whether flood insurance will be required by a lender.

Florida has standardized building codes throughout the state that substantially increase the ability of a home or building to withstand high winds. During recent hurricanes, newer homes sustained far less damage than the older homes. Mobile homes usually sustain the most damage from high winds of any type building, although changes in their construction required by new building codes has dramatically increased the strength of the new ones. Florida also has a program where anchors can be installed on older mobile homes free of charge to help keep them from being blown away.

If you want to enjoy all the good things that Florida has to offer, you have to accept the fact that hurricanes are a reality that you have to deal with but by choosing locations and buildings wisely, hurricanes can be little more than a temporary inconvenience.

The southern half of Florida has a tropical climate. This means that it's going to be warm and humid throughout the year. Since there is a lot of dampness and humidity, most homes will be CBS construction. This means they are built with concrete blocks covered with a cement or stucco exterior coating. This type construction is less prone to dry rot and termite damage. In the north half of Florida you will see a lot more wood frame construction.

When talking about the south half of Florida we can't forget about the Florida Keys. The Florida Keys are a series of islands that start about 15 miles south of Miami and extend southwesterly approximately 150 miles to the city of Key West which has 32 percent of the entire population of the Keys. The total land area of the Keys is only 137 square miles. The Keys divide the Atlantic Ocean to the east from the Gulf of Mexico to the west. If you like island living and love to fish, the Keys might be for you. Real estate can be expensive and it is always best to get together with a real estate agent who knows the Keys and can give you all the pros and cons concerning the lifestyle and values.

The east and west coastlines of Florida are very different. The east coast from Jacksonville south obviously has the Atlantic Ocean. There are beautiful brown sand beaches all the way south to Miami which has led to heavy development all along the coast. The Atlantic Ocean is very deep just a short distance from the shore which made it very easy to create deep water ports in Jacksonville, Cape Canaveral, Ft. Pierce, Palm Beach, Ft. Lauderdale and Miami. These ports cater to the cruise industry and cargo delivery. The Atlantic Ocean also offers an abundance of deep water fishing and diving opportunities. Beautiful beaches and lots of recreational activities including the Daytona Beach racing activities, draw a lot of people to the east coast. Because the Florida east coast is very densely populated and developed, the prices of real estate are normally higher than most other areas of Florida.

The west coast of Florida is different. The Gulf of Mexico water is shallow along the west coast with only Tampa having water depth sufficient for Port and cruise ship operations. From Naples north to Tampa there are beautiful white sandy beaches. From Tampa north to the Florida panhandle area, the shoreline consists of mostly small islands and mangroves. Beaches through this area are usually man-made. There are a lot of rivers and lakes along this stretch of coastline that are created by the many fresh water springs that produce many millions of gallons of water each day. The area is world famous for the manatees that like to congregate in the warm spring water during the winter months. There are a lot of small towns along the northwest shoreline of Florida and it is considered rural.

The northwest Florida panhandle area has beautiful white sandy beaches which are certainly equal to any other area of Florida. However; because of its location further north, the weather gets cold during the winter months, therefore summer is the tourist season for this area while the rest of Florida enjoys a winter tourist season.

The center part of Florida offers a variety of terrain and real estate opportunities. Starting at the south is the Everglades. The Everglades basically is a swamp that is mostly public land and will never be developed. The Miami area relies on it for a lot of their water supply. As one moves north you travel through a lot of farm land south of Lake Okeechobee that is used primarily for raising sugar cane. Lake Okeechobee is located in the center of the state south of Orlando and is the 7th largest fresh water lake in the U.S. covering over 730 square miles. There are several small country towns around the lake that rely mostly on the cattle and agriculture industries for employment.

The land north of Lake Okeechobee is used largely to raise cattle. Northwest of the lake is the City of Lakeland which is the center of the phosphate industry. There are a lot of phosphate mines on the south side of Lakeland. They also rely heavily on the citrus industry. Lakeland is a popular location because it is located on Interstate 4 between the cities of Tampa and Orlando.

Orlando is located right in the center of the state and is the number one tourist destination in the world with Disney World, Epcot, and Sea World among the leading attractions. Orlando's central location makes attending the attractions a reasonable drive from almost anywhere in Florida. The rapid growth of new communities all around Orlando also makes it a favorite relocation area for foreign buyers.

The north central part of Florida is mostly agricultural with a lot of small towns where real estate is relatedly low priced compared to the rest of Florida.

We've given you a very brief thumbnail description of Florida. Because of the size and diversity of the state, there's something for everyone. The state is fairly narrow so it's usually a comfortable drive from anywhere to any of the major attractions or the coastal areas. When considering the purchase of real estate, the metropolitan areas are growing the fastest because that is where the most of the employment opportunities are located so that's where the prices will usually be the highest. The ideal situation for a lot of people will be to find a home close enough to a big city to take advantageous of everything it has to offer such as shopping, recreation, entertainment, restaurants, medical facilities etc. but still be far enough away to avoid the congestion.

Here are some of the really foolish things people do when choosing a location to purchase a home:

Buying near an airport: Florida has a large number of airports. They all play a vital part in the economy. People buy homes around the airports and then suddenly realize that airplanes fly in and out. They make noise and even occasionally crash. These people then run to city and county meetings and complain about the noise etc. Fortunately they usually receive very little sympathy.

Buying on a busy street or thorough-fare and then complaining about the traffic: You can't complain about 24 hour traffic and noise if you purchase a home on a busy street or near a major highway or turnpike. This can also create dangerous situations for families with small children. It also affects the resale value of the home.

Buying next to a convenience store or other 24 hour businesses and complaining about traffic and noise: People who shop at convenience stores sometimes tend to be noisy. Drinking beer and congregating in front of a store is common. There is noise and traffic 24 hours a day. There can be a lot of debris around a store and some store properties are unsightly. This can devalue residential properties around these types of businesses.

Buying next to a school and complaining about the kids: If a person doesn't like to be around kids, buying next to a school is not a very good idea. There will be a lot of traffic from parents dropping off and picking up kids. There is usually a lot of noise during play time or around sports practices and games. There can be meetings at night and sports events with bright lights.

Buying on a river or lake and complaining about boats: If you purchase on a lake or river that allows recreational boating, there will be noise from boats, water skiers, jet skis, fishermen, etc. Water can be dangerous if you have small children. Property taxes, insurance and property maintenance will usually be higher. On the other hand, there is only so much waterfront property so values can be much greater.

Buying in a declining neighborhood: There are a lot of reasons why homes in a given neighborhood decline in value. A new shopping mall could be built on the opposite side of the town or city causing local neighborhood retailers to shift to the new location leaving a lot of vacant stores and local retail space. This always hurts the overall value of a neighborhood. New highways can do the same thing. Populations tend to shift to newer more convenient locations.

Neighborhoods can decline in value because of age. Older homes tend to be smaller and many times less quality was put in to the construction because many were built before strict building codes were introduced. Smaller older homes many times tend to be turned into rentals which can cause the decline of a neighborhood. Lack of deed restrictions or local control can also cause a decline in values.

Location, Location, Location: Location is critical when purchasing real estate. The whole point here is, think about these things **before** you purchase, not after.

5

MISTAKES PEOPLE MAKE

If you can't afford it, **don't buy it!** During the recent hot real estate market we saw many people invest in all kinds of properties that they simply couldn't afford. The recent collapse of our economy and the real estate market can be blamed to a large degree on lending institutions and governmental programs that encouraged people who had no cash or credit to purchase real estate. There were mortgages that had low monthly payments in the beginning but then escalated over a short period of time to a point where the buyer could no longer afford the monthly payment. Mortgages were created for amounts higher than the property value. People over paid for commercial properties and vacant land because the real estate market was so strong that everyone thought the "boom" would never end.

Read the fine print. It's amazing how many times we have heard people say, "I really didn't understand what I was getting in to." "I thought I would make money." "They told me I would make money." "I should have read the contract or mortgage." In the

State of Florida, when you sign a purchase contract and it is accompanied with something of value such, as a cash deposit, **it is enforceable.** That means that you can lose your deposit and you can be sued for non-performance if you default on the contract. Both the purchaser and seller are bound by the terms of the contract. Ignorance is never an excuse.

Beware of mortgages that escalate. There are several types of mortgages out there. That's why it is critical that you understand what you are signing and that you read the fine print. A lot of people with poor credit were offered mortgages that began with a low interest rate and a low monthly principal and interest payment. That sounded great but after a relatively short period of time the mortgage started escalating, the interest rate started going up and with each increase in interest the monthly payment went up. The payment went up to a point where many families could no longer make the payment resulting in the Lender foreclosing on the property.

One of the other mistakes people make is to forget about monthly fees that may be required in addition to the mortgage payment. These can be homeowners insurance, property taxes, HOA fees and CDD fees. The lender is going to estimate the annual insurance payment and property tax bill and collect approximately $1/12^{th}$ of that amount each month which will be added to the mortgage payment. Depending on where the property is located, this can substantially increase the monthly payment. The Lender will pay the property taxes and insurance at the end of each year to make sure the property is always insured and also to prevent a tax lien from being placed against the property. Property taxes and insurance historically have usually gone up over time which can also increase the monthly payment each year. Also remember that if you purchase a condo or a home in an area that has a Home Owners Association, (HOA) there will be monthly or yearly fees payable to the Association. If a development was created through the use of a Community Development District bond program, (CDD) then responsibility for repayment of the bond can be passed on to the homeowners and that fee will be added to the annual property taxes. A good real estate sales person should be able to provide a list of all the required fees associated with the purchase of a given property.

When purchasing real estate, you should always have an exit strategy. Most people put no thought into an exit strategy. It's not something that is pleasant to think about but what happens if you have an emergency such as a death of a spouse or loss of a job? Can you sell the property? A lot of people retire to Florida and purchase a home and then one spouse passes away. The remaining spouse decides that they want to move back up north to be close to their family. Can they sell the home and recover their investment or will they have to take a loss?

If you are operating a business, do you have enough cash reserves to weather a financial downturn and loss of business? For example, the restaurant business has the highest failure rate in the country. There are a lot of reasons why restaurants fail such as poor location and inadequate parking, but one of the major reasons is the fact that people go into the restaurant business and spent a lot of money purchasing the real estate, equipment, signage etc. and have no cash left to make it through the "start-up" period. It takes time to establish any business. If one does not have the cash reserves to make it through the first year then that business is probably going to end up on the failure list.

Proper planning with an exit strategy can prevent a lot of problems.

According to a very interesting recent survey, 39 percent of recent homebuyers said that they would buy a different size or different priced home and in a different neighborhood knowing what they know now. This confirms what we have known for a long time. Buyers make too many emotional decisions instead of taking the time to do the research and gather the information that will help them make more intelligence real estate investments. Any buyer new to an area needs to do his or her homework. We encourage buyers to use real estate salespeople who know and have intimate knowledge of the whole general area not just the small community where they live. It always pays to use "professional" real estate salespeople and take the time to do the research.

This is particularly true with people who are being transferring in to a new area to a new job or job location. They are many times forced to make quick decisions regarding commuting distances to the new job, placing their kids in good schools, the accessibility to medical facilities, etc. Sometimes it's better to rent for a short period of time rather than make a quick decision that you regret later.

A Special Note Concerning Contracts:

We hear stories from people who made an offer to purchase real estate and failed to get the property they wanted because they were totally unaware of the legal responsibilities of all parties and how the process works.

Under Florida law a contract is very difficult to enforce in court unless it is accompanied by something of value such as a deposit. Binding contracts must be <u>fully executed</u>. That means that both buyer and seller must sign the contract and initial any and all changes. A seller is not obligated to accept any offer even if it is for the full sales price. A seller can get several offers and he has the right to accept or counter on any one of the offers. Being the first to make an offer doesn't entitle a potential buyer to anything.

If you are working with a real estate salesperson, the law requires the salesperson (unless he or she has power of attorney for the seller) to present all offers to the seller regardless of the offering price or conditions. A buyer also has the right to withdraw an offer any time prior to the notification back to the buyer that the seller has accepted the offer.

A word of caution! We have heard stories of buyers who made offers on more than one property and had all the offers accepted. That means they just bought more than one property. If they put up a deposit with each offer, they have binding contracts that can be enforced in court. We've also heard stories of sellers making counter offers on more than one offer and the counters were all accepted. They just sold their property to more than one buyer. These situations can turn into legal messes. A good real estate salesperson would always advise his or her clients to avoid these situations.

Should personal property be included in a contract? No! Lenders will not loan on personal property. Personal property should be handled separately and you should use a Bill of Sale agreement. By personal property we mean furniture, lawn mowers, bicycles etc. Appliances, ceiling fans, lights, washers and dryers, window coverings are considered part of the real estate and would normally be included in the real estate purchase agreement.

Marlin Realty & Investments, Inc.

Verbal offers mean very little to anyone and are basically a waste of time. If you are unsure of where you stand in any given situation regarding the preparation or presentation of an offer to purchase real estate, we would recommend that you <u>seek proper legal advice.</u>

6

FOREIGN INVESTORS

During the last few years, foreign investors accounted for about 15 percent of real estate transactions in Florida. Orlando is the 19th largest market for foreign investments in the U.S. and the largest in Florida. The Florida real estate market is diversified with a relatively high turnover which provides fairly easy exit options. There are few barriers to property ownership and foreign investors have basically the same rights as American property owners.

If we were advising a foreign investor, the first step would be to develop an investment plan with an exit strategy. What is the purpose of your investment? What do you want to try to achieve? How long do you want to hold the investment? Are you looking for income producing properties or just a second home? If you are looking for income producing properties, we would recommend that you use a real estate profession and an attorney who is accustomed to working with foreign investors. Don't expect to get legal advice from real estate salespeople unless they are also attorneys.

If you don't have a green card or an American social security number, you may find that it is difficult to get a loan. If you are able to find a lender, you can expect to pay a higher interest rate and they will usually require a higher down payment. Some of the other issues to consider are the currency exchange rates, locations that are convenient to international transportation facilities and locations that are convenient to major Florida tourist attractions.

The major airports that handle international travel are Miami International and Fort Lauderdale International located in southeast Florida. Orlando International located in central Florida and Jacksonville International located in northeast Florida near the Georgia/Florida state line and Tampa International is on the West Coast. The northwest Florida panhandle has a new airport near Panama City called Northwest Florida Beaches International Airport that opens the Florida Panhandle and its beautiful white beaches to international visitors.

Please note: For foreign investors wanting to permanently move to the USA, unless you were born in the USA, or marry a U.S. citizen, or you are the minor child or parent of a U.S. citizen, or buy or start a business (under strict guidelines), or invest in a legally recognized project which will give you a visa such as the EB-5, or are lucky enough to find a U.S. employer who will go through an extreme hassle to employ you, then we understand that it will be very difficult to legally move here.

Those seeking permanent residency need to seek the advice of a good immigration attorney. Requirements can be rather complicated and expensive.

Also we understand that there is confusion among some foreign investors regarding Florida property taxes and the Florida Homestead Exemption Law which exempts property taxes on the first $50,000. of the assessed value of a homeowner's permanent residence.

Under Florida law, the homestead exemption is only available to U.S. citizens, permanent resident aliens or others who are legally able to form the intent to remain permanently under immigration laws.

Marlin Realty & Investments, Inc.

7

TYPES OF INVESTMENTS

Let's take the most common types of real estate investments and address them one at a time.

Vacant land and lots: Is purchasing vacant land or lots a good investment? It depends on what your investment goal is. Purchasing land and lots for the purpose of flipping for a quick profit requires a lot of expertise and knowledge of what is happening in the marketplace. If the prices are going up and the area or location is "hot", (high demand) then you can usually purchase and re-sell at a profit. However, if you buy at or near the top of the market and the market abruptly changes and goes down, then you can take a serious financial loss. You have to stay on the right side of the curve. Also be aware that vacant land can be very difficult to finance. A lot of banks will not loan money on vacant land.

If you buy land with the goal of building a home or commercial building on it, then you would want to try to purchase at a low cost in most instances. Location is critical but you also have to remember the 80/20 rule - eighty percent to the improvements and twenty percent to the land. The 80/20 rule will not necessarily apply for commercial property since location can be the most important factor.

When purchasing vacant land there are a lot of questions that need answers. What is the zoning for the property? Does the property have to be re-zoned? Are utilities available to the site? Are highway improvements required? Is the land located in a "flood zone"? How much on-site water retention is required? What are the parking requirements for your intended use? Is fill required and how much? The list goes on and on and that is why you need professional help particularly if you are purchasing land for commercial purposes.

Single Family Home: When purchasing a single family home there are a lot of things to consider. Is the home going to be a permanent residence or a second home? Second homes are much more difficult to finance and maintenance and security can be a problem if it stands vacant for a portion of the year. It is probably better to purchase a second home in a gated community where maintenance, lawn care and security are available. Before buying a home, consider whether it's within a neighborhood where properties are likely to retain their values. With a retirement community, take a close look at the community's financial condition. Most banks won't give loans if the mortgage delinquencies in a community with a Homeowners Association exceed 15% or, if 25% of its homes are unoccupied.

If you are planning to purchase a home for a primary residence, you have to determine whether you want a previously occupied re-sale or a new home. Location will often times determine what you purchase. The neighborhood or development you are interested in may already be completely developed and the only homes available may be re-sales. If you purchase a home in an age restricted community (55 years of age and up), will you have difficulty selling the home a few years down the road. You have to remember that when you want to sell, the age restriction limits the pool of potential buyers for the home.

If you are interested in buying or building a new home, here are some things that you have to consider.

If you want to build your own home, you can act as your own contractor and sub out the work. This can save you a lot of money or it can be a nightmare if you don't know what you are doing. If you have no building experience, we recommend that you hire a general contractor to do the work and closely monitor his progress. Finding a good well located building lot at a reasonable price will also be an issue. Is it in a flood prone area? Does it have utilities available etc.? There are many questions that have to be addresses when determining if a vacant lot is suitable to build on.

If you want to purchase a new home, there will be many new developments around all of the metropolitan areas of Florida. There will be two types of builders. The first will be the "tract" builder who will usually offer only three or four different floor plans for a given development. By restricting the number of floor plans along with the colors of paint, tile and carpet choices, the builder can keep his costs down and offer the homes to the public at a lower cost. This does not mean that you are getting an inferior product. There are many national and local tract builders who build outstanding homes and stand behind their products. The second type of builder is the "custom" builder. The custom builder will design and build to the customer's specifications. Because they are customizing everything, they will usually be much more expensive and the homes tend to be larger and on larger lots.

Buying a new home offers many advantages. Let's look at some of the most obvious. In the 1990's Florida had several hurricanes that caused so much damage that several insurance companies left the state. As a result, Florida saw the need to create a state wide building code that was adopted in 2002 that requires builders to greatly improve the strength and wind resistance of the new homes. Each county is allowed to add to and improve the statewide code every three years. Most counties, especially those along or near the coastlines have aggressively improved the statewide building code to the point that we now have some of the strongest building codes in the nation. Simply put, when you buy a new home in Florida, you get a stronger home, a better roof, better windows and superior insulation. And, everything is under warranty for the first few years. This usually results in lower insurance rates, less maintenance, lower utility bills and higher values over the long run. Also most of the newer communities have superior amenity packages such as swimming pools, club houses, tennis courts, golf courses and gated security. The price of a new home with builder incentives is often very competitive with the cost of purchasing a previously occupied home.

A mobile home or manufactured home is also an alternative. Some areas have deed restrictions against these types of homes and they also usually sustain the most damage during a hurricane. It is always wise to purchase a newer model that has been built using the new building codes and one that is properly anchored.

Condominium: Technically, a condominium is a collection of individual home units along with the land upon which they sit. Typically, a condominium consists of multi-unit dwellings such as an apartment building or a housing development where each unit is individually owned and the common areas such as swimming pools, hallways, recreational areas etc. are jointly owned by the Homeowners Association. The Homeowners Association, through its elected representatives, manages the common areas and each individual owner pays a monthly fee.

Condominiums can be apartments or detached homes. One of the things a buyer of a condominium has to understand is that the Homeowners Association controls what the owner can and cannot do through their rules and regulations. Strict rules and regulations are usually designed to protect the value of the homes and apartments. A condo is probably the best investment for a part-time resident or a foreign buyer because all the maintenance and security is usually provided by the association.

Commercial Property and Business Opportunities: A commercial property can be any type of property that provides an income for the owner. The use of a commercial building is determined by local zoning codes. The location of the property usually determines the usage. Retail zoning for instance is usually located along major thoroughfares where businesses can get maximum traffic exposure. Zoning laws vary from community to community. Purchasing any type of commercial property requires a lot of research and planning.

Many small businesses fail each year. There are several reasons for a business failure but a couple of the primary reasons is poor location and inadequate parking. Location and adequate parking is critical to any business so when you purchase a commercial property always factor that into your research.

A business opportunity does not necessarily involve the purchase of real estate. One can purchase a business and rent space. Purchasing a business opportunity can be risky and requires a lot of expertise and analysis. The biggest problem is trying to determine what is fact or fiction when examining the books of a business. If you are not an expert in the particular business you are looking at, seek the advice of an expert. Also it is very wise to have a reserve fund that enables you to stay in business for at least a year while you are building the business.

We're going to continue to stress that proper planning with an exit strategy will pave the way to opening and operating a successful business.

8

FINANCING

This is a tough subject to address. Since the economic downturn in our economy and the government "bail out" of banks, we now have a new ball game. There are new rules, new regulations, new attitudes and new uncertainties that we now have to deal with. Whether you think this is good or bad, this new situation has created some incredible real estate opportunities.

If you have excellent credit, you can be in a good position to take advantage of a depressed real estate market, however if you have a marginal credit score or a poor credit score, it's going to be very difficult to get a mortgage. Banks have all tightened their requirements and are increasing the amount of cash that you have to put in to the transaction. With changes in the Federal Truth and Lending Act, lenders are examining buyer's credit under a microscope. Banks usually use a FICO credit score to determine whether a buyer qualifies for a mortgage. Scores range from 300 to 850. Higher is better.

If you have marginal or poor credit, you can rebuild or improve your credit score by doing a few simple things. Always pay your bills on time. One late payment can significantly reduce your credit score and may also increase the interest rate if it is a credit card payment. Keep your credit cards to a minimum. Every time you apply for a store credit card it can lower your credit score even though you don't use it. Keep the credit card ratio low (the amount you owe as to how much your credit limit is). A credit counselor can strategize steps for clearing up inaccuracies and improving credit scores.

Save for a down payment. Buyers will need more of their own money to buy a home. A good down payment shows ability to pay and will usually give you the best interest rate on the new mortgage.

If you are looking for financing, it is always better to go to the bank or banks where you already have a credit history. It can be easier to get the loan, the interest rate and terms can be better and it can save time. You should also get a pre-qualification letter from a lender. This letter will state the maximum amount of money that you can borrow. Most sellers will ask for a pre-qualification letter when you present an offer to purchase so that they don't waste time with someone who cannot qualify to purchase their property. It also gives you an idea of what you can or cannot purchase. We are constantly amazed at buyers who want to look at homes that are priced beyond their ability to finance.

Financing commercial property or projects is a much different process. Banks usually have commercial loan departments and personnel that specialize in commercial lending.

There are federal loan guarantee programs available such as FHA and VA or USDA loans.

An FHA insured loan is a Federal Housing Administration mortgage insurance backed loan which is provided by a FHA approved lender. FHA insured loans are a type of federal assistance and have historically allowed lower income Americans to borrow money for the purchase of a home that they would not otherwise be able to afford. Since FHA does not make loans, the first step in obtaining an FHA loan is to contact several lenders and/or mortgage brokers and ask them if they originate FHA loans. As each lender sets its own rates and terms, comparison shopping is important in this market.

VA loans are guaranteed by the Department of Veterans Affairs and can be used by qualified veterans to purchase or build a home. Veterans can qualify to put zero down on a loan up to $417,000. Again it's important to contact several lenders and/or mortgage brokers and ask them if they originate VA loans

USDA loans were introduced in 1991 by the U.S. Department of Agriculture (USDA). They were designed by the government to assist medium income Americans living in rural areas to purchase a home. For borrowers who meet certain requirements, the program offers lenient approval requirements, very competitive interest rates and a minimum down payment. Requirements will vary from area to area so anyone interested in this program should consult a mortgage broker.

Purchasing and Financing Foreclosures: Let's first determine the difference between a "short sale" and a bank owed home. A "short sale" takes place when a home owner and their mortgage holder agree to sell the home for a price that is below or "short" of what is owed on the mortgage. Short sales are difficult to deal with because there are three parties involved - the buyer, the seller and the lender. Offers are always subject to the lenders approval and lenders usually have their own contract forms that favor the lender. These contract forms many times give the lender the right to cancel the contract if a higher offer comes in from another buyer. Short sales can sometimes take weeks to get answers from lenders and months to close.

A bank owned home is when a lender forecloses on a home and the courts give the lender a deed to the property. These are referred to as REO homes. (Real Estate Owned) These homes are usually easy to work with and just as easy to finance as any other home unless the home is partially finished or there is substantial damage to the home that the lender does not repair. The lender will usually get a current appraisal of the property which normally would take into consideration the physical condition of the property. They then will usually price the property close to the appraised value. Many times a bank will consider financing their REO properties. It pays to ask.

Many bank owned properties are placed on the market at below market values simply because the bank wants to get them off their books. However it would be a mistake to think that the bank is going to accept an offer of 50% or less of current market value. We see people passing up great buys simply because they think they are going to find a "steal". Banks are limited as to how much of a loss they can write off. In today's market, finding the so called "steal" is going to be the exception rather than the rule. Greed often times causes a buyer to pass up a tremendous real estate investment.

When dealing with a bank owned property a buyer has to understand that it is a "numbers game" with the bank and not an emotional decision when they consider an offer to purchase one of their properties. If the bank cannot accept an offer, they will usually counter offer at a price that they can accept. In today's poor real estate market, when a bank forecloses on a property, they usually have to take a loss in order to sell the property but again, there is a limit as to how much they can accept below current market value.

Owner Financing: Beware of owner financing! There are many reasons why an owner would offer financing. Most often it is because he can't sell the property. Seller terms may sound good but the seller usually does not want to wait long term for all his money so there probably will be a "balloon" payment involved. We recommend careful examination of the conditions involving owner financing and we recommend the use of an attorney.

Marlin Realty & Investments, Inc.

9

PROFESSIONAL ASSISTANCE

Don't ever assume that a person with a real estate license in his or her pocket knows anything about real estate. There are over 360,000 active real estate licensees in Florida. All one has to do is take a License Law Course, pass the course and then take and pass a State written exam and "bingo" you're a licensed real estate "expert". You can then put that license with a licensed real estate broker or builder and make a ton of money selling real estate. The truth is, very few real estate licensees make a substantial amount of money. A lot of real estate sales people are what we call "order takers". They sit in an office and wait for someone to call or walk in the door and ask to purchase or sell real estate. They have very little expertise outside of the community where they live or where their office is located. Since purchasing real estate is usually one of the largest investments a person makes in their lifetime, finding that investment should require more than the assistance of an "order taker".

Marlin Realty & Investments, Inc.

For several years we located sites and built stores for one of the largest retailers in the United States. The retailer would direct us toward a city or town where they wanted to locate a new store. We would then go to that town or city, research the market, locate the competition, determine where the growth areas were, do the demographic studies, meet with governmental officials and then locate the three best available sites. Working with the retailer, we would determine which site best met their criteria, place it under contract, purchase the site and then build the store. To save time, we always tried to find a real estate broker or salesperson familiar with the area and who had expertise relating to zoning, governmental regulations, market trends, available land, etc. In most cases, we had to do all of the research ourselves because local real estate brokers or salespersons with that kind of expertise simply didn't exist.

However, with that being said, we want to stress that there are a lot of good knowledgeable professional real estate salespeople in every area of Florida. You simply have to find them. If you are unhappy with the salesperson you meet, then find someone else. A good real estate broker or salesperson should have knowledge of the entire area where you want to locate to or invest in. If you are looking in a given county in Florida, the salesperson you work with should have knowledge of every community within that county, be familiar with pricing, growth areas, vacant land and lots, commercial activity, taxes, zoning and governmental fees and development requirements. The more experience the salesperson has, the better.

A good real estate salesperson will usually belong to a Board of Realtors® that has a Multiple Listing Service (MLS). Every member of the board will place their real estate listings in the MLS. Everything is computerized and organized so that it is very easy to identify property by category and by location. Once a salesperson understands what a buyer is looking for, they can very easily identify everything that is on the market that fits the buyer's needs. Buyers who try to find properties on their own usually miss a lot of what is on the market. Some sellers do not want "for sale" signs on their property and some communities limit "for sale" signs. Many times buyers miss good bargains simply because they don't know about them. The MLS can also provide information concerning what properties are selling for in any given area. The Multiple Listing Service provides a wealth of information that the salesperson can share with the buyer so that he or she can make an informed and wise investment.

The computer has drastically changed the way real estate is bought and sold. Today, a real estate salesperson has to be completely familiar with the Internet and all the tools related to it. A laptop, electronic notebook and a printer are essential tools for a successful salesperson. In years past, a person looking to purchase a home would stop into a real estate office, meet a salesperson who would find out what he or she was looking for, look up homes on their MLS and make appointments to show the buyers homes that fit their criteria. Now, a buyer doesn't have to go to a real estate office. Most people have a personal computer that they can use to search for homes through the Internet. By using sites such as Realtor.com, Zillow and Trulia, a buyer can focus on an area where he or she wants to locate to and get a general idea of home values and what is currently for sale. We say "general idea" because sites such as Zillow and Trulia are not always completely up to date. It sometimes takes them a while to catch up to the local market changes. Local MLS systems are constantly being updated so the most accurate information will come from the local real estate salesperson.

Since we have moved into the "computer age", local newspaper classified advertising used for selling real estate has dropped dramatically. Magazines advertising homes for sale that you used to pick up at the local supermarket are going out of business. The computer has allowed buyers and sellers to become more "savy" about real estate which is a good thing. Good real estate sales people find that it is easier to work with more informed customers.

Note: If you decide to work with a real estate salesperson, please remember that the salesperson usually does not get paid for chauffeuring people around to look at properties. Unless there is some other arrangement, the salesperson only gets paid when there is a successful sale and purchase. After working with a salesperson, if you find a property that you like, don't run to a friend or relative who happens to have a real estate license in their pocket and have them present your offer. This will create problems and may land your friend or relative before the Grievance Committee of the local Board of Realtors®. Always work through the salesperson you are working with and let them do their job. That's the fair and ethical thing to do and it will always work out to your advantage.

When you invest in real estate, you may need the assistance of a number of professionals so let's go down the list.

Civil Engineers: If you are involved in building or developing commercial real estate or residential developments, you're going to need the assistance of a Civil Engineer. In the United States, only a licensed engineer may prepare, sign and seal, and submit engineering plans and drawings to a public authority for approval, or seal engineering work for public and private clients. An engineer's work must also comply with numerous other rules and regulations such as building codes and legislation pertaining to environmental law.

Civil Engineers work closely with surveyors and specialized civil engineers to fit and serve fixed projects within a given site, and terrain by designing grading, drainage, pavement, water supply, sewer service, electric and communications supply, and land divisions. Civil engineers are typically involved with geotechnical engineering, structural engineering, environmental engineering, transportation engineering and construction engineering. They apply these principals to residential, commercial, industrial and public works projects of all sizes and levels of construction.

In any given area there is usually a small group of Civil Engineering Companies that do the majority of the engineering work for that area. They normally have offices in the areas and are very familiar with local governmental requirements and local political climates. You have to remember that building codes and governmental requirements will vary from county to county and city to city. Using a Civil Engineer who is familiar with all the local issues can save time and money

Surveyor: Surveying is the process by which a surveyor measures certain dimensions that generally occur on the surface of the Earth. A survey is used by Civil Engineers and contractors to design from and build on. Boundary surveys are usually required by lending institutions to determine if there are any encroachments on the property and to make sure that everything is correctly located. Also elevation surveys may be required to determine if the property is located in a flood hazard area. Civil Engineers usually have survey teams on their staff. When developing raw land, surveys are used to lay out streets, drainage areas, utilities, highways, infrastructures, etc.

Attorney: When investing in real estate it is always wise to use an attorney; however, it is critical to use the right kind of attorney. We would highly recommend that you always use an attorney who specializes in real estate. There are many horror stories about people who use a friend or relative who is an attorney but who has no experience in closing real estate transactions. Those closings can turn into real night-mares.

In every area there are usually several attorneys who specialize in helping developers obtain the required governmental approvals for their project. These attorneys are usually well versed in local and state laws and issues pertaining to development of real estate. They are familiar with the local political issues and can guide the developer throughout the entire approval process. A good real estate attorney can make a developer's life much easier.

Architects: An architect is a licensed individual who leads a design team in the planning and design of buildings and participates in the oversight of building construction. Since architects make decisions that affect the safety and well-being of the general public, they are required to obtain special education and experience to obtain a license to practice their profession. License requirements will vary from state to state. An architect must thoroughly understand building and operation codes as well as understand the various building methods that are available in order to produce the best possible results for the client.

General Contractor: A General Contractor is a group or individual that contracts for the construction or renovation of a building, road or other structure. General Contractors are usually licensed by the State. Every builder, whether residential or commercial, will have someone on the staff that holds a general contractor's license. A General Contractor should be able to show a license and proof of insurance.

Title Companies: A title company will perform an "abstract of title", which involves searching the real estate records of the county where the real estate that you are purchasing is located. This abstract of title will determine who the legal owner of the property is and reveal any mortgages, liens, judgments or unpaid taxes that have to be satisfied before the property is conveyed to the buyer. It also will detail any existing easements, restrictions or leases that affect the property.

After the abstract is completed, the title company will issue an "opinion of title" or if title insurance is to be issued, "a Commitment of Title Insurance" which will be given to the lender and/or buyer. The title opinion letter or title insurance commitment will set forth all things that need to be completed and any problems that need to be corrected before the purchaser can receive "good title". Once everything is completed, the Title Company prepares a "Closing Statement" which outlines all the costs associated with the transaction and then the buyer and seller can exchange the paperwork and "close" the transaction. After the closing, the Title Company will take the legal documents to the county courthouse where they will be date stamped and then recorded. It can take up to two or three weeks for the recording and then the original documents will be returned to the correct parties.

The title insurance policy protects the buyer from any future claims against the title to the property. It's always wise to get title insurance.

Bankers: Every bank usually has a Special Assets Department.

This department has the responsibility for disposing of the bank's "toxic" or special assets which would include foreclosed properties. Some banks put people in charge of the Special Assets Department that have little or no real estate experience. In that case it is usually very difficult to complete a real estate transaction. On the other hand, some banks employ experienced real estate "professionals" who make it easy to complete a real estate transaction. It's been our experience that the larger banks tend to have the largest number of inexperienced individuals handling their real estate sales.

It's always wise to seek the help of a good real estate attorney or a good real estate broker when dealing with bank owned properties or "short sales".

Mortgage Brokers: Mortgage brokers are licensed professionals who are paid a fee to bring buyers and lenders together. They are usually independent contractors who work with many different lenders. They evaluate a buyer's credit to determine which lender is the best fit for the buyer's needs. They may present applications to several lenders. Mortgage brokers can sometimes find a lender who is willing to make a loan even though the buyer has had a loan application rejected by a bank. Commercial loans are sometime easier to find when using a mortgage broker.

Mortgage brokers are licensed by the State of Florida.

Appraisers: Real Estate Appraisers determine the value of real property and what it would sell for considering current market conditions. Appraisers must be licensed by the State of Florida and must meet experience requirements. Lenders use appraisers to determine if the loan they are making on a property is justified by the property's market value. Some appraisers are directly employed by lenders while others work as independent contractors.

Marlin Realty & Investments, Inc.

10

QUESTIONS MOST OFTEN ASKED

Here are some of the questions that we're heard most often over the years.

Q. **Why are there very few basements in Florida?**

A. The majority of land in Florida is relatively flat and the land elevation is not very high above sea level which means that the water table is going to be close to the surface.

Q. **What is a "short sale"?**

A. A "short sale" takes place when a lender agrees to the sale of a property for a price that falls short of the actual amount owed on the mortgage.

Q. **Do I have to use an attorney or can I use a Title Company** to close the purchase?

A. You can use either one. They both can close a real estate transaction. We would never advise anyone not to use an attorney especially if it is a complicated commercial transaction. If you feel comfortable using an attorney then use one but make sure that the attorney is a real estate attorney who is accustomed to closing real estate transactions.

Q. **Why are there very few double paned windows in homes in Florida?**

A. Cost. Most builders don't put them in because they cost more. Double paned windows provide better insulation and can help reduce utility bills.

Q. **What's the difference between a tile roof and a shingle roof?**

A. They are both good roofs. A tile roof is more expensive to install and maintain. Concrete tile roofs are used on the more expensive homes. Tile roofs reflect the heat and are used more often in South Florida where you have warmer weather year-round. Tile roofs have to be pressure cleaned periodically and repainted to prevent the build up of mold and mildew which can cause the concrete to deteriorate.

Q. **Do wood framed homes withstand hurricane winds better than a concrete block home?**

A. Experts tell us that wood framed homes can withstand a little higher wind because they are a little more flexible; however more stringent building codes have made concrete block homes much stronger so there isn't much of a difference now.

Q. **Why are "open" floor plans so popular in Florida?**

A. Florida has mild weather year-round so everyone wants to open up their homes and bring "the outside in" as much as possible. Open floor plans allow the fresh air to flow more freely though out the home.

Q. **Should I purchase a home that is on a septic system?**

A. If you purchase a home where there is no public sewer system then you have no choice. There is nothing wrong with a septic system that is well maintained. Purchase contracts usually have an inspection clause in them that allows you to check out everything. A septic system inspection would be highly recommended. Florida has gotten a lot more restrictive concerning septic systems which will make them more expensive to install and maintain.

Q. **Why do some homes have orange stains on them that look like rust?**

A. A lot of people have shallow water wells drilled to be used to water their lawns. The water from shallow wells, particularly in South Florida, can sometimes have a high sulfur content which when sprayed on walls or walk ways leaves an orange stain. The only way you can prevent this is to install a water filter system.

Q. **How long does a typical roof last?**

A. A typical roof will last 20 to 25 years depending on how well it is maintained.

Q. **Should I buy a home with a lawn irrigation sprinkling system?**

A. Florida lawns need to be watered on a regular basis. Sprinkler systems are more efficient and can be put on a time clock. A good irrigation system can save you money in the long run.

Q. **Should I be concerned about settlement cracks in the home I'm considering for purchase?**

A. It depends on the cracks. There will be some hairline cracks, which we also refer to as "spider" cracks, in almost any home that has been built on a concrete slab. Spider cracks are not serious. If you see cracks that are large enough to drop a penny into, we would recommend further inspections.

Q. **Should I use a Building Inspection Service when purchasing a home?**

A. Yes. If you are purchasing a previously occupied home it is always wise to use an inspection service. Make sure the inspection service is licensed and insured. Most purchase contracts will address this issue and will specify who is responsible for repairs. New homes should have warrantees.

Q. **What does CBS construction mean?**

A. Concrete Block Stucco. Most homes built with concrete blocks have exterior stucco or cement coatings which are usually painted.

Q. **What kind of contract should I use to purchase Florida real estate?**

A. If you are working with a Realtor®, he or she will usually use what we refer to as a "FAR/BAR" contract which is a form contract developed by the Florida Association of Realtors® and the Florida BAR Association. These contracts are usually more than adequate for purchases of residential real estate and the blanks can be filled in by the real estate salesperson. If you are working with an attorney or purchasing a more complicated commercial property, then the attorney will probably prepare the contract. We would never recommend going to a business supply store and purchasing a form contract. Those contract forms usually never offer the protection that you would need.

Q. **What is Chinese drywall?**

A. Chinese drywall refers to defective or tainted drywall imported from China from 2001 to 2007 that emits sulfur gasses which usually creates a noxious odor and corrodes copper and other metal surfaces. There are also claims that it causes adverse health effects. A good building inspection service can determine whether it was used in a home.

Q. **Can I buy real estate through an auction?**

A. Yes. A savvy investor can make a profit buying through an auction; however, research is the only way that one can yield real auction dividends. You should know the value of the property. You should know if there are any liens, unpaid taxes or fines. You need to know the motivation of the seller and what the reserve is. And, most important, you need to look at the property before you bid. Auction companies should be licensed and they usually post on- line the rules and conditions of the auction.

Q. **If I am trying to purchase a property and I am competing with other offers, do I have the right to know what the other offers are?**

A. No! A seller is under no obligation to share with a potential buyer any information regarding a competing offer. It would also be unethical for a licensed real estate salesperson to share any information concerning competing offers. The only time you are entitled to know what the other offers are is when it is a legitimate auction conducted by a licensed auctioneer.

Q. **How can I find out how long a property has been on the market for sale?**

A. If you are being represented by a real estate salesperson, that person should be able to answer the question because most multiple listing services post that information.

Q. **If I purchase real estate, do I have to attend the "closing"?**

A. No. The attorney or title agent can do what they call a "mail away". Documents can be mailed or E-mailed to buyers and sellers. We live in the "electronic age".

Q. **Are there age restricted communities available to me if I don't want to be around families with children?**

A. Yes. There are a lot of communities throughout Florida that restrict age to 55 years and up. They are usually designed to provide activities that appeal to retirees. Many have tennis courts and golf courses where residents can play free of charge. Most have guard gate security.

Q. What are the advantages of buying a new home?

A. This is not an easy question to answer because there are so many variables. Age, location and condition of any home have to be given serious consideration; however, let's look at some of the most obvious advantages to purchasing a new home in Florida. Florida has some of the strictest building codes in the nation. As a result, when you buy a new home in Florida, you get a stronger home, a better roof, better windows and superior insulation. And, everything is under warranty for the first few years. You usually will have lower insurance rates, less maintenance, lower utility bills and higher values over the long run. Also most of the newer communities have superior amenity packages such as swimming pools, club houses, tennis courts, gated security etc. and the price of a new home with builder incentives is often very competitive with the cost of purchasing a previously occupied home.

Marlin Realty & Investments, Inc.

ABOUT THE AUTHORS

Buck Boyles graduated from Glenville State College with a Bachelor of Science Degree in Education and also earned a Master of Science Degree in Education from West Virginia University. Buck has over 30 years of experience in Florida real estate sales, development and home building. His high level of real estate experience has placed him in the unique position as a "problem solver". If a buyer or seller has a problem, Buck can usually resolve it quickly because he's usually already had experience with the situation. Buck is currently serving as Vice President of Marlin Realty & Investments, Inc.

Preston Boyles grew up in the real estate business. He graduated from Florida State University with a Bachelor of Science degree in Management Information Systems. In addition, he graduated from East Central University with a Master of Science Degree in Human Resources. His sales expertise and computer knowledge has quickly allowed him to become a top producer and leading expert in the real estate business. Preston is currently serving as President of Marlin Realty & Investments, Inc.

Marlin Realty & Investments, Inc. is located in the Greater Tampa Bay area of Florida. The authors can be contacted by visiting their website at **www.marlin-realty.com** or sending an email to **book@marlin-realty.com**.

www.ingramcontent.com/pod-product-compliance
Lightning Source LLC
Chambersburg PA
CBHW071801170526
45167CB00003B/1124